My Mother's Journey with Cancer

Poetry by Dr. Saroj Daulat Ram
with Dr. Sonia Anand

Copyright © Sonia Anand, 2020

All rights reserved.

Cover art: Dr. S.V. Anand

ISBN: 978-1-989403-17-4

To contact author:
66 Bay St South, #612
Hamilton, Ontario
L8P 4Z6

Email: sonianand@gmail.com

Editorial assistance: Avery McNair

Layout & Design:
thepublishingmentor.com
inourwords2008@gmail.com

Contents

About the Authors ... 4

Introduction ... 7

Chapter 1: Coming to Canada ... 10

Chapter 2: Cancer Diagnosis—A Shock ... 18

Chapter 3: Cancer Returns ... 20

Chapter 4: What is the Look of Cancer? ... 24

Chapter 5: No Turning Back from a Relentless Cancer ... 28

Chapter 6: Living with Cancer, Thinking about the End ... 39

Chapter 7: Final Days ... 43

Chapter 8: The Pain of Cancer is Relentless ... 46

Chapter 9: Winter of Life's End ... 49

Chapter 10: Mother's Wish ... 56

Chapter 11: Angels ... 61

Epilogue ... 63

About the Authors

SAROJ DAULAT RAM was born on May 6, 1930, in Jandiala Guru, Punjab, India. Her mother died when she was a year old, and Saroj was raised by her grandmother.

In 1939, Saroj moved to East Africa to be with her father and new step-mother. In 1947, she moved to Nairobi to begin senior Cambridge schooling. She finished first in class, and although her father thought it was time for her to get married, he gave in to her wish to go to medical school instead. She attended medical school in Mysore, India and then continued on to the Royal College of Surgeons in Dublin, Ireland.

In her final year of education in Dublin, Saroj met a dynamic moral re-armament speaker, Dr. Sundaram Vivek Anand, a true believer in Gandhi's principles. She thought Anand to be a kind and intelligent young doctor. Soon after, on the 24th of October 1960, Saroj Ram and S.V. Anand were married in London.

The happily married couple set out for Ibadan, Nigeria, where Saroj received a job in the pediatric emergency room, and Anand worked as a surgeon. Here, she frequently saw patients suffering from typhoid, tetanus, and malaria; the neonatal mortality rate in Nigeria at that time was 50 percent, and thus she was very grateful her first pregnancy went smoothly without her being afflicted by similar diseases. It was a difficult job.

In 1961, their first daughter Gitanjali was born in Nigeria, and in 1965, Saroj and Anand courageously moved to Kentville, Nova Scotia in Canada, where medical doctors were needed at the time. Saroj and Anand worked at the Blanchard Fraser Memorial (BFM) Hospital, Saroj in anesthesia and Anand in surgery.

In 1967, their second daughter Anita Indira Anand was born, followed soon after by daughter Sonia Savitri Anand. Gita, Anita, and Sonia attended King's County Academy in Kentville and grew up happily; the family integrated well into the small-town East coast lifestyle.

In 1985, after 20 years in Kentville, Anand and Saroj moved to Napanee, Ontario, where Anand worked as a surgeon. Saroj started a residency program in psychiatry at the Kingston General Hospital, and then returned to Halifax, Nova Scotia alone to start up a counseling practice. While living there, she was diagnosed with cancer, so she closed her practice, and moved back to Napanee.

Saroj and Anand moved to Georgetown, Ontario in 1995, where Saroj retired and Anand continued to work as a surgeon.

Saroj had a great interest in poetry and created a women's poetry group in Georgetown, which met once a month. She was an active member of the University Women's Club of Georgetown.

As a mother and grandmother, she was very present and devoted to family life. Her three daughters and grandchildren lived fairly close to her home and visited her often.

Dr. Saroj D. Ram is the author of several books, listed below:

A Tribute to Gandhiji, IOWI, 2011; 978-1-926926-06-4

Songs of Praise Based on the Bhagavad Gita, IOWI, 2011/revised 2017; 978-1-926926-10-0.

Tulsi Ramayan, IOWI, 2013; 978-1-926926-24-7

Daily Prayer Lifelines, IOWI, 2013; 978-1-926926-25-4

DR. SONIA ANAND is Dr. Saroj Ram's youngest daughter and is also a physician by profession. Sonia trained in medicine at McMaster University. She completed a vascular medicine fellowship at the Brigham and Women's Hospital in Boston, United States, and her Master's and PhD degree in research methods at McMaster University. Today she is a Professor of Medicine and researcher at McMaster University. Dr. Anand holds a Canada Research Chair in Ethnic Diversity and Cardiovascular Disease; and the Heart and Stroke Foundation Michael G DeGroote Chair in Population Health. In 2019, Dr. Anand was inducted into the Canadian Academy of Health Sciences.

Dr. Anand lives in Hamilton, Ontario, with her husband and three children.

Sonia Anand with her mother, Saroj Daulat Ram

Introduction

Breaking the news of the death of a loved one to a family member has always moved me in its profoundness. It is delivering a message of finality like no other. For much of my medical career and life, I could only imagine the grief and loss I was initiating for family members of the deceased. Reflecting back on my years as a physician, I found the impact of breaking such news to families was monumental, be it in the emergency room, in the intensive care unit or in the convalescent ward. It was jarring, emotional and sometimes it was a spiritual moment—always it stayed with me for days afterwards. I felt the pain of the broken earthly bond between mothers and their children, a break like no other.

When I sat with my own beloved mother, helping her up from her chair and up the stairs; holding her from behind so she wouldn't fall backwards; changing her dressings; trying with each activity to minimize the pain she experienced – I realized the end of her brilliant life was near. Through it our powerful bond was deepening. In a few short weeks in November 2014, before her death, I could feel her incredible strength gradually slipping away. Nothing could prepare me for this time in my life, and nothing has been the same thereafter.

Losing my mother was the most difficult reality I have ever faced. Perhaps unrealized in that first half of my life, I had a safe haven in my mother's advice, her prayers and love.

Now, as I witnessed her suffering and slowly dying, I felt helpless. I was overcome by a full recognition of how often she had held me up, had my back, and in many mysterious ways navigated my smooth ride so far. I could not reconcile with the fact that in these final days of her life I could not help my mother more. I had offered hope and cure to many patients. I had guided families through this process of a loved one's death many times. But now, as a daughter, I was helpless.

My mother, Dr. Saroj Ram, passed away on November 20, 2014 at the age of 84, after a seven-year struggle with breast cancer. She battled through a mastectomy, lumpectomy, radiation to both breasts, her pelvis and spine. She had taken oral chemotherapy for her final year-and-a-half of life.

As an avid poet, she shared her unique perspective on her life in general and journey with cancer specifically in a collection of poems. She wrote from her vantage point as a physician, spouse, mother, grandmother, and a deeply spiritual person.

This is the story of my journey with my mother through her terminal illness. It tries to capture the incredible courage and faith by which she accepted her fate. In her writing and in mine, I hope our experience rings true for others and provides some comfort. Too many of our loved ones have had to walk this devastating path.

Sonia

My Mother's Journey with Cancer

Chapter 1

Coming to Canada

My mother had immigrated from India to Africa to rural Nova Scotia, Canada, in 1965. She trained as a medical doctor well before it was common for a woman to attend medical school. She had a conviction that studying medicine would give her independence from the traditional expectations of an Indian woman, and indeed it did.

Her love for her patients was evident from her early years as a practicing physician in Ibadan, Nigeria, where she had a job in the pediatric emergency room. There she frequently saw patients suffering from typhoid, tetanus, and malaria. Although the job was very difficult, it was also rewarding. It also made her ever grateful for the birth of her first healthy daughter, Gitanjali in 1961. In 1965, after hearing the call that physicians were needed in Canada, she and her husband Anand took jobs in the small town of Kentville, Nova Scotia. Saroj worked at the Blanchard Fraser Memorial (BFM) Hospital in anesthesia and also made house calls as a family doctor in New Ross, a town a half-hour drive away. Anand, her husband, worked as a surgeon in the same hospital and together, the couple affected many of the town's families, saving many lives. The early years in Nova Scotia required her to adapt to a new country, culture, and climate. However, Saroj loved her clinical work and she loved her family life. She lived passionately, starting an Indo-Canada group during her years in Nova Scotia. Towards the end of her life, she started a poetry group in Georgetown, Ontario.

Throughout her life, Saroj kept copious notebooks, jotting down observations, writing poetry, her thoughts and feelings regarding life in Canada. This was the journaling of an immigrant woman's practice of medicine in small town Nova Scotia, and her hopes and dreams for her three daughters. Although sometimes feeling disconnected from her cultural traditions, Saroj loved

Canada, its beautiful four seasons, the endless opportunities the country offered to immigrants and in particular to her family.

Canada

I love thee too
My adopted land
In thy warm embrace
Happily, I stand!
I love thee with fervour anew
Basking in the Golden Hue

But far away from home
There is another land
India my motherland
I love her too
More than can be understood
She is poor and bent with age
Long time ago she had her golden age.
She was proud and wove a golden shroud
Invaders small and great
Looted her golden age
They left her poor and naked
Poor and forever outdated
But I love her still
Love that time shall never kill.

Canada my adopted land
I love thee truly while
I pine for that Indian land
I leave my children in thy care
Take care when I am no longer there!
These two mothers I have
One old and culturally great,
One new and humanly great.

Saroj loved her work as an Anaesthetist, putting patients to sleep before their surgery and caring for them afterwards in the recovery room. Work was not without its challenges; her writing shows she was sometimes caught in battles between physicians. Also, as an Indian female physician in rural Canada, she was subjected to prejudice. She struggled with this, but kept going through her faith, love of Canada's beauty and opportunity, her love of medicine, and obligation to her patients.

Her passion for her work and her commitment to her patients is highlighted in her poems, as exemplified in the following piece:

1981: Nova Scotia, Prayer for my Patients

I pray to you my God
Always let me do the best
For my patients
Rendered to my care
In sacred trust
Almighty God you know
That with absolute Honesty
I do perform my Duty
To those who entrust
Their lives in my care!
Each life is sacred
And I treat it as such!
Please God allow me to work
Always as long as I live
My best I shall Give
To them so that they shall Live!
In the nature of Curse
And with method sure
I will not blind them
And give them false Hope.
God allow me to carry on
I shall give them the best of Honest Trust
O God your honest Help is
In thee we trust!
Amen

Her Husband—and my Father—Anand, was her life partner and clinical associate. He was an energetic optimist, who saw the world as hopeful and full of promise for his family. He worked incredibly hard, taking night calls constantly for surgical emergencies and learning new skills to bring back to his local hospital. Although he was always tethered to the hospital, he found time to take his wife and three daughters on ski adventures and cottaging at their ocean house. They hosted elaborate dinners and parties for friends and neighbours.

After some political uncertainty within their local hospital, Anand decided to pursue additional training in public health, with the hopes of changing career paths. He hoped to take on a Global Health role. It was a difficult time for the family with two of the daughters still in high school and my mother, Saroj continuing to work in the politically-charged hospital environment.

Saroj wrote of Anand as he left Nova Scotia to begin a Master's Degree in Public Health at Johns Hopkins in 1981:

Anand

Your work here is done
The heartaches have begun
It's time for you to go
Seek your fortune anew
When work is no more a pleasure
There is nothing to hold you here!
But the memories shall always be there!
For it was here that our children were born
And here they took their first steps
And held our hearts in their little grips!
Here they went to school
To learn Life's rule!
15 best years of your life
Have just slipped by
Now go seek your fortune
In the houses of learning
Let knowledge fulfill your yearning.
I shall keep the home fires burning
When you are new things learning
Let this chapter now be closed
And rid our minds of its load.

As a physician and citizen in Canada, my mother held the public health care system in high regard. It was never more felt by her than when she herself became ill and needed the services of the system; so is it for many of us. Here, she captures her feeling at the end of her days regarding life as an immigrant in Canada: was she right?

Health Card

Went to renew my health card
It would be my last.
As in the queue I stood
In ethnic shroud
In multi-racial hue
Blacks and yellows
Whites and browns
Blonds and brunettes
All had equal place
No bias of race
Tears welled in the eye
Had a silent cry
Coming to Canada was right
Land of Charter of Rights
Forever, may it stay
The unbiased way.

Chapter 2

Cancer Diagnosis—A Shock

In 2008, my mother was awaiting a routine cataract surgery and I was by her bedside. In her blue hospital gown, she said, "Sonia, I think I have a lump here in my left breast." Under the sheet I palpated for it and to my utter shock and dismay indeed there was a lump. It was not small, but I reassured her I would set up the appointments. While she was in surgery, I set to work arranging an ultrasound and biopsy at my home hospital in Hamilton.

That evening I was scheduled to give a talk to a women's group on hormone replacement therapy. I had to inform them of the risks of health conditions including breast cancer, and the benefits of the post menopause treatment. It was a tough evening, trying to be strong and counsel other women while simultaneously trying to digest my mother's likely cancer diagnosis. I cried to and from the talk, all the while going through my upcoming presentation in my mind, with my mother's words ringing in my ear, reinforcing her strong Hindu beliefs, "You must be strong, Sonia, and do your duty."

These words would play through my head many times in the months and years to come. The journey with cancer had begun.

Between the biopsy diagnosis and working through receptor positivity and actuarial tables, the doctors suggested that my mother should undergo a mastectomy, the removal of the breast with the cancerous lump, followed by radiation therapy. She was prescribed oral chemotherapy with a drug called tamoxifen.

Outings

Visiting I do much
To a doctor's as such
My cancer to recheck
From clinic to clinic
In specialist's office sitting
No cure for cancer yet
Delaying the inevitable end
Is all they can do
In the end, cancer gets you
Draining the energy out
Aches and pains abound
Ambition is no longer around,
A quick unexpected ending
Will, indeed be a blessing.

Each step of treatment was very difficult, but my mother faced them stoically and overall remained quite well over the next two years. In April 2011, back pain indicated that the cancer had spread to her bones.

Chapter 3

Cancer Returns

May 2012

I stood with Mom and watched the ultrasound. It was definitely a circumscribed lump, this time in the breast which had originally been cancer free. The young radiologist announced: "it is malignant, we just need to confirm with a biopsy."

Wow, that stings, to hear the matter of fact, life-changing pronouncement by the recently-qualified radiologist. Perhaps he knew I was a physician and felt he could speak more freely or with more technical jargon. Or perhaps he was so young and had never been on my side of the bed holding a loved one's hand and did not think twice about his announcement.

I squeezed Mom's hand while the doctor froze the area and performed the biopsy. Note to self: empathy is learned, and professional skills, including trying to be empathetic, must be taught. I wondered how many other family members learned of their loved one's fate in this cold, clinical manner. I recalled my medical school communication skills training regarding how to deal with different types of patients: the angry patient, the depressed patient, and even how to deliver bad news to a patient. I also thought back to my mother's empathy when I was ill or sick, her service, and her concern.

My thoughts turned to this young radiologist doing this job day in and day out, not hesitating to talk of 'cancer' or using the term 'malignant' without pausing to think or feel the impact of his pronouncements on the patient.

My Mother was very stoic, as always, perhaps not revealing to me how she felt hearing this devastating news. In my frustration, I reminded myself that my role was to be strong for her, and keep it together, reversing the mother-daughter role to daughter-mother. Sometimes as a griever you start anticipating grief and its impact on *yourself*. In this case, I was truly saddened for my

Mother *herself*. She had done so well keeping the cancer at bay and carrying on with her daily routine. This was indeed a huge setback and we both knew it.

The doctors told us we would find out the final results the following week. After the procedure, my sister, Mom, and I had her favourite grilled cheese sandwich before leaving the cancer centre. It is always so nice to be together even under such gloomy circumstances. It is being together, sharing laughs, holding each other up that is truly the essence of life.

July 2012:
Approximately one month after the pre-op appointment with the breast surgeon, my Mother underwent surgery to remove the new breast lump at the hospital where I worked day in and day out. Thankfully, she was discharged from the hospital the same day and recovered well. She stayed with me so I could care for her through the early post-operative course.

That night Mom stayed at my home just outside Hamilton, and all of the grandchildren came and visited with her while she sat on the big L-shaped couch in the living room. We watched *My Big Fat Greek Wedding* together and had popcorn with lots of butter and salt, a family favourite.

We now awaited the oncology team's decision as to whether Mom should undergo radiation as an adjunct to the surgery. That would be a new challenge, but my Mother took this news with grace and stoicism. Together, we welcomed the brief reprieve between a successful surgery and news regarding next steps. Life for my Mother, my Father, my sisters, and me returned back to normal.

August 19, 2012:
My youngest son, my Mother's youngest grandchild, who she had jokingly suggested I name Grant, because I always seemed to her to be writing a research grant, celebrated his 9th birthday! We had a lovely celebration today at our country house. We had our entire family over to celebrate his birthday. My sisters and their families came to our place, and we were blessed with beautiful August weather.

As my parents age, to have all of us together is a blessing! The grandchildren played music and soccer, swam, and ate desserts together. I tried to spend as much time with my Mom and Dad as I could, while also directing traffic and serving as host for the afternoon. I reminded Mom how she was with me for each of my children's births, including Sachin, who we were celebrating today. We recounted how she would be doing her crossword puzzle during the delivery, playing her Indian music, and walked to the McMaster bookstore to buy some Gandhi books. I told her how lucky I felt to have that memory. She told me she was lucky to have me and that I was more than what a son could bring to them, which, in Indian culture, is a huge compliment! Of course, this was making me teary as we reminisced of old times.

Mom read the famous *The Prayer of Francis of Assisi* to my son and me, which we will always treasure as a guide for us. We had a lovely sunny day, brilliant company, positive loving energy. I wish time could be suspended in that blissful peacefulness.

The Prayer of St. Francis

Lord, make me an instrument of your peace,
Where there is hatred, let me sow love;
Where there is injury, pardon;
Where there is doubt, faith;
Where there is despair, hope;
Where there is darkness, light;
Where there is sadness, joy;

O Divine Master,
Grant that I may not so much seek
To be consoled as to console;
To be understood as to understand;
To be loved as to love.

For it is in giving that we receive;
It is in pardoning that we are pardoned;
And it is in dying that we are born to eternal life.

~ St Francis of Assisi

February 2013:
My Mother came through four weeks of radiation like a hero. Although the sessions themselves were brief, the travel time for her was an hour by car. Usually she was driven by a cancer volunteer from her home in Georgetown, Ontario. The driver would pick her up, drive her to the appointment, wait for her during the session, and take her home. Each time she would bring a Toblerone or Swiss chocolate bar for the driver to show her thanks. Given that my parents were both in their 80's, this volunteer service was a huge blessing for which our entire family was grateful. A small service, quiet soldiers, who provided a listening ear and helped time pass during difficult journeys.

    I met my Mother each day with a wheelchair at the front door of the hospital before her appointment to help her to the radiation suite. I often had to leave early from the hospital in which I worked to rush to the cancer hospital to be there before Mom. She wasn't a 'texter,' so my Father would send a text once she had left, and I would time it so that I would meet her at the front entrance. After she got changed into her hospital gown and we waited, she would pick up the knitting left by hospital volunteers for patients. Collectively, patients and their families would knit squares for quilts that would be used to comfort cancer patients in the nearby hospice. My Mother was not at that stage (yet) and felt she was contributing to the comfort of others by picking up the yarn. I would fumble my way through knitting alongside her, getting stumped on the 'knit one pearl two,' and she would correct my mistakes.

    When she was called in for radiation, the procedure took just 15 to 20 minutes, and then she would return from the suite and get changed out of the hospital gown. Then we would proceed to the little café beside the radiation suite for tea and either the requisite grilled cheese sandwich or a Kit Kat bar shared together. At first Mom handled radiation treatment fine, but slowly her energy level dropped. I was sorry that the radiation was so tough on her, and she responded saying that even though it was daunting to get ready every morning for the three-hour round trip, she looked forward to meeting me every day to chat and spend this time together; it was the highlight of her day, she said.

Chapter 4
What is the Look of Cancer?

At my Mother's monthly appointments at the hospital, we would sit and wait together. We had wonderful conversations about my Father, our relatives, my work and stories of her past – lots of laughs, always.

On one of these days we sat together in the waiting room of the lab and looked around – my Mother (as a physician) whispered to me that some other cancer patients looked so gaunt and weak. I agreed, then looked at her and saw the same look on my Mother's face. Later that day, I wrote my thoughts and fears in this poem:

What is that look, that look of cancer?
>Will I have it too one day?
>My Mom spotted it in the waiting room,
>We thought she was ok.
>I was too afraid to tell her
>That I spotted it too,
>This time not on a stranger
>But in her,
>My most beloved Mother.
>With this sighting
>I became sad for her,
>Scared for me,
>And angry at this disease,
>Which robs one's health
>And steals their joy.
>
>We'll beat this look,
>We won't allow it to take my Mother's beauty,
>We'll stay positive,

Ignore it,
Remain close,
Laugh it away.

But despite all of this,
It persists,
It haunts us,
Unspoken,
We feel our precious time together
Slipping away.

What is the look of cancer?
Why do so many people struggle
To stop it in its tracks,
With little avail,
For when the look of cancer is present,
All implicitly acknowledge that the end is near.
The gaunt faces,
The stare of pain,
The listless affect,
The loving relative beside.
This is the look of cancer that haunts me now.

My Mother's doctor says firmly, "the cancer is going to kill you. You will die of cancer."

We look down at the floor, my Mother says, "hmm hmm, so this is not a cure?"

"No this is not a cure," says the doctor.

These words sting and ring loudly in my head for hours and days later.

My Mother is stricken with a fatal disease – we all sit together in a cold hospital room.

My loving Father's eyes well up with tears, as do mine now as I write this.

How impossible is it to envisage not having my Mother, which would break up our family?

I cannot.

Hearing the prognosis that afternoon given to my Mother so definitively by her oncologist was jarring for my Father. As a life-long optimist it was crushing for him to hear the news of an abruptly terminal journey. Ironically, as a surgeon who had treated many breast cancer patients, he had given similar prognoses to countless patients in the past. However, when it is you and your closest soul mate, time stands still, and you long to return to the comfort of your home and resume life as normal.

My Father asked me again if he is sure he heard the oncologist correctly?

"Not much time left," I say, we acknowledge this in our despondent stares.

After this jolt, my Father decided to stop working. He had quite a career for someone of 82 years who gave to his patients selflessly and even worked through his own diagnosis and treatment with cancer four years earlier. Now he said he would devote his time solely to caring for my Mother. My Mother managed fairly well after radiation, even resuming her favourite activity: convening her ladies poetry group every month at her home. She provided tea and hot snacks, and the group members would also bring treats, sit together, compose poetry, and read it out to each other. Often throughout my Mother's journey with cancer she would be sure to schedule her cancer appointments around her poetry group meetings, and not the other way around.

Here is one such poem that she wrote in her poetry group while she was facing cancer. There were many friends of my Mother's who would visit or call her and tell her about a new cure for cancer, be it Ayurvedic medicine from India, a certain food to eat in large quantities like asparagus, or a tincture of Holy water. My Mother listened, and sometimes even tried these, as conventional medicine was not keeping the cancer at bay.

Alternate Medicine

They tell me—
Bone cancer can be beaten
If organic food is eaten
With flaxseed bread.
Drink juice of berries red,
To smoothie add flaxseed oil
Your veggies to only par-boil
Ground seeds of apricot
Add to your cereal bowl
Almonds or sunflower seeds
One must chew indeed.
Any animal protein or fat
Is taboo in your diet
Forget not the carrot juice
With drop of basil-oil in juice
Eating asparagus every day
Keeps the cancer away.
Nature cure is the new rage
When modern medicines fail
In your cottage cheese
Sprinkle some flaxseed.
Spirulina for extra energy
Nature cure is worth a try
When chemo, radiation fail
And death your body claims
But cancer is a wily customer
Mutates like wayfarer.

Chapter 5

No Turning Back from a Relentless Cancer

Towards the end of June 2013, our family attended the 50th anniversary party of Mom's dear friends from East Africa who had similarly been resettled in Nova Scotia and then later in Ontario.

For the occasion, Mom and Dad and my nuclear family rented adjoining rooms at the Marriott Hotel by the airport in Toronto, and it was great fun as we all got dressed in our best Indian outfits, going back and forth between rooms. Mom was choosing between her saris asking each of us for our opinion on the best one – she opted for the South Indian silk over the black Shimmer.

Down at the cocktail party, my Mother met a lot of her old friends and had written a poem for the event. When the time was right, I helped her up on stage, and she read her heartfelt poem for her friend. It was one of the highlights of the night.

Untitled

May God shine his light
On all your lives, very bright
May in its lustre your lives glow
Forever and ever and now
Your friendship is worth gold
From our days of old
From Kenya and Agra
From Nova Scotia in Canada
Feel privileged to have known you
Like kith and kin, are you
Stronger than blood ties
Your nature so generous and kind
Always there when in need
For your friends indeed
Robin and Sanjay, you have done
Us all proud, I say it aloud
What a beautiful family to behold
Under the blessings of god
Lord has showered His light
May it continue to be bright
This comes from our hearts
May you always tread the noble path
That you have done so far
Loyalty to friends is your hallmark
Write a few tips for folks like us
Who by your friendship are wonder-struck
Enriching qualities to pluck
You two noble souls,
As good as gold
A joy to behold
Our dear friends of old.

Afterwards the children enjoyed some dancing but slowly all the other family members left, my Father going to bed early and my sister going home. It was my wonderful Mother who wanted to stay and dance the Bhangra! As she said, "You can't keep a Punjabi from dancing Bhangra!" She had a wonderful evening of dancing. We finally left the party at midnight, tired but happy.

The next morning, I got up early before the kids and brought some tea and coffee up to my parents adjoining room. Mom and I enjoyed talking and having tea while Dad and the boys slept. It was a great debrief on the night, and on life in general, and given her love of biographies and history, a bit of Roosevelt thrown in there too! After our buffet brunch, I helped Mom and Dad with their bags. A wonderful family event indeed.

July 2013:
A few days following this wonderful event, which is imprinted in my fond memory bank, my Mother, who rarely complained, called me to tell me she had severe pain in her right leg. At first it was controlled with Advil but soon a burning pain set in, and the only relief was to lean forward; it had the sound of nerve root pain. I optimistically thought the pain could be caused by a herniated disc brought on from the Bhangra dancing or carrying out the garbage. As I talked it over with my Father, we realized Mom needed some tests.

In quick succession, after discussing with her oncologist, I met Mom and Dad at my hospital for plain X-rays; Mom was in such pain. The results of the X-ray came back inconclusive, and her oncologist arranged for a special CAT scan. My poor Mom had a wince on her face, and she told me the pain was worse than that of childbirth. The Advil and nerve medication were not taking the edge off the discomfort – Nobody should suffer that much! One day later I received a copy of the CAT scan report, and upon reading it, I was overwhelmed with grief.

The cancer had spread to her lungs, liver, and bone. This news bowled me over – it felt like receiving a body blow. The CAT scan revealed an aggressive cancer. I could not call my Mom to give her such news over the phone. Overcome with grief, I rearranged my schedule, and barely being able to see through my tears, I drove the hour to my parents' house.

Trying to endure my own sadness, I spent the drive talking to my sisters on my speaker phone while working up the courage to tell my parents. When I arrived, my Mom looked over at me, knowing already why I had uncharacteristically driven to her home on a weeknight, and asked me point blank about the result; I told her the bad news. She said she suspected this, for nothing else could cause such pain.

From my impression of my Mother, she was very strong and tough and did not easily or ever cry when given bad news nor in the final days when she had so much pain. However, as a Mother myself I know that a Mother tries to protect her children, to give them the best advice, to prepare them for life when she can no longer care for them. Thus, I may not have known what my Mother was truly feeling about her disease, as she was likely trying to protect us from massive grief and worry and minimize the pain we experienced. We are grateful to have her poetry; a day was not fulfilled for her unless she had written. Here in her poems we see a glimpse of her feelings:

Cancer is in my Bone

Now the cancer is in my bone.
I live on miraculous hope
That tamoxifen will do the trick
To evict the cancer with big stick,
Or the virgin's mantle
Will hopefully handle
The cell
From my flesh to expel.
Without hope, there is no cure
But do I want to live more
If my strength is gone?
Bed-ridden is anathema to me,
Mental confusion is not for me.
I want to go before
Confusion takes hold,
Before depression mars the life
With daily bodily strife
Death comes to all,
When heavens finally call
All your medications will fall
At death's open door
Be ready for the final knock
By God's set clock.

My Father was in shock, one sister was in denial, and the other was overwhelmed by the news. That night as I went to pick up my son from his soccer game in Brampton (because life must go on!), I made some calls and emails to arrange for Mom to be seen by the oncologist the following morning. The oncologists at the hospital were able to arrange emergency radiation treatment: one big dose to the lumbar spine and pelvis with the hopes she would get some pain relief. Once again, she asked if this treatment would "cure" the cancer that had spread to her bones – but of course it could not.

Waiting for the planning and radiation was hard on Mom,

not only was she in tremendous amount of pain, but she developed esophageal spasm from the Advil she took on an empty stomach. At her request, I got her some milk and the antacid Tums and she settled a bit before the radiation. As we waited through her discomfort, she reviewed with me (again) the steps on how to knit with the yarn and knitting needles in the waiting room.

The radiation didn't take too long, but afterwards Mom felt sick, and had to wait for me to get the car. She really was a pillar of strength, incredible to me how stoic she was through that time. Unfortunately, my Honda Civic wasn't the smoothest of rides and by the time we got to Georgetown from Hamilton my Mom felt very nauseated and almost ready to throw up. She sat down on her chair in the living room, and we gave her some Gravol. I left shortly after as my sons and husband were leaving the next day for a soccer training camp in Atlanta, Georgia.

Mom insisted on giving me a fifty-dollar bill and said she couldn't repay me enough for all I had done – of course I only did what any loving daughter would do. I hated to see my Mom suffer so much. That night I prayed that the radiation would at least give her some relief from the pain.

July 2013:
My sister and I went with our Mother to her follow-up appointment regarding the spreading cancer. She was prescribed some new treatment for pain and a new oral chemotherapy drug was recommend, but we all noticed the new lexicon used by the oncologist. Words like "palliative," and when I asked about her best-case scenario for how long my Mother had to live, she said about six months.

Putting a time limit on the most influential person in my life was surreal. My sister and I teared up, but Mom stayed firm: "there is always hope," she said, "everyone's time comes." Not even a quiver. She showed us how to be real fighters and we began a new chapter of hope, that she would continue to stay strong through the chemotherapy and not have too many side effects. It was impossible to imagine life without my Mother as she was always such a rock of wisdom and strength and advice.

That night when I called her, she said to me, "Thank you for everything. Cheer up!" Me, cheer up? She stands for everything good and kind in this world, and I am truly lucky, truly blessed to have had such an incredible Mother. She worried about my Father and how he will manage alone, as do I, and I wonder how we will all change, and how much we will miss her when she is gone. I hugged my kids longer that night. I am so grateful that they each got to know and meet their Grandmother and hold a part of her within them.

August 2013:
My sister Anita and I visited with Mom today, sitting together on her couch in Georgetown, with the car-chase movie, *American Bandit,* starring Burt Reynolds and Sally Field playing in the background. My cousin from England, whose own father had died of cancer, had written me a very nice email that I wanted Mom to hear. Anita read the touching words out loud to Mom and as Anita started to tear up at the kindness of the note, my Mom exclaimed, "Oh look at that car!" Mom wanted to maintain her usual routine, and our moping around and wanting to talk about her cancer didn't change her mind.

Mom is better on the morphine, she went to see her garden; the flowers, beans, and zucchini amazed her, as did the giant weeds. I spent the past three days with her while my husband and kids were cottaging and camping. It gave me time to stay with Mom and Dad and help at the house. I see her struggling to do housework and walk upstairs. My sister Anita and I try to help without being too intrusive. She goes to bed at 9 pm and reads her all-time favourite biography of Queen Victoria. She awakens at 6:30 am and plays spiritual music, does her crossword puzzle in *The Globe and Mail,* takes her meds, and has *a lot* of telephone calls and visits with friends.

September 2013:
We held a family prayer gathering at Mom and Dad's house today. The Hindu Priest from the temple came and said prayers and sang Indian spiritual songs called Bhajans. Mom spent the early part of the day preparing her house for the event. I was amazed

at her new-found energy! When I arrived, she was dressed, having already cleaned the kitchen and prepared sweets. Together we put marigolds from my garden in the prayer area and set the couches up, burned incense and then prepared the samosas and tea for later. We had two hours of rest before everyone arrived at 4 pm.

We prayed to bring blessings to Mom and Dad and their home, we honoured them, and prayed for them. Mom blessed all the grandchildren. The house was crowded with relatives and friends, and my parents' home had a real glow and warmth to it.

At the end of the afternoon Mom was tired, but I could tell she loved the gathering; she loved to entertain, she loved to give people gifts of chocolate, she loved the prayers said together. For this we are so thankful, for the day, for each miracle, for each smile, and for minimal suffering. When I left the house that evening, I was happy to have helped Mom feel so content, and of course she came to the door to wave goodbye, and thanked me profusely, despite how tired she was.

October 1, 2013:
For my birthday today, I was blessed to have Mom and Dad visit me and the family at our home. Mom hasn't been here since Thanksgiving last year and has not seen our new renovation. It was a glorious day of fall; warm wind, and beautiful fall colors. We drove here after my Mom's appointment at the cancer clinic, and she seemed quite comfortable and in no hurry to leave. We talked about fall: it is both of our favourite season with so many contrasting colours. Dad was already waiting in the driveway when we arrived home, having taken pictures of our house for a painting we want him to create.

We went inside together and had crackers, cheese, samosas, hummus and tea, and I opened presents from Mom, Dad, and the kids: chocolates, books, lots of beautiful cards. Mom rehabilitated my plants (as she always did) by taking some cuttings and watering them, transplanting some old ones into new. We took family pictures together on the back deck.

Later, when they left, my eldest son walked Mom out to the car, taking care on the gravel. A blessing for me to have my Mom here on my birthday – the best present of all!

Birthday Poem for my Daughter

Heart of our heart, soul of our soul
Our promise and our hope
By giving us a gift of you,
God made our dreams come true.
You are our crown jewel,
Our magnificent angel.
From the day you opened your eyes
Born with wisdom of the wise
You were self-sufficient even as a child.
Loved reading fairy tales all the while
Using long English words as a child,
Amusing us with your winning smile.
Many accolades came our way
When you won academic honours by the day.
A prayer rises from my heart today
May the lord guide your step each new day,
May he give you a brilliant future,
And warm you with his merciful nurture,
May all your hopes and dreams come true
As the lord did ours by the birth of you.
We wish god's choicest blessings on you
As your life's ideals you pursue,

April 2014 Easter: A Family Affair
Many times throughout the last year, I wondered if ever I would be privileged to host my parents again and the whole family at my house for a big family celebration. In fact, I had already mourned the loss of that privilege on multiple occasions—last July for my sister in-law's 50th birthday, last August for my youngest son's birthday, last Thanksgiving, last Christmas. Now, thank heaven, we are all able to be together to celebrate Easter with the Grandparents. That was a blessing.

Each of my children had to make something for the day, my youngest chose a poem, my middle child, a fruit salad, and my eldest, the classic trifle. My Mom and Dad took their rightful places at the head of the room and loved to see all the grandkids filing back and forth enjoying being together. We ate, took photos, read poems, chased the dogs, went for a walk, played soccer, a marvelous day was had by all.

I wish I could capture that moment and bottle it up, but I know I can only add it to the memory bank for future – to get me through hard times.

June 2014
Mom has now developed right-hip pain. In the waiting room of the cancer clinic, Mom walked by herself to get her blood test. She read my palm. She said I have a very good headline but not a strong money line. She needs another X-ray and CT scan. She is staying strong, talking of her love-hate relationship with England. I love spending time with her in this way, yet hated to see her suffer.

Cancer, No Time to Waste

I have no time to waste
Between cancer and me
Is a deadly race
Cancer is over-taking me
Insidiously it is creeping
Into every organ seeping
A pain here
Or an ache there
Galloping, tentacles pinching
Now here, now there
Rigor in hot weather scenario
Like rigor of malaria
General well-being is gone
Never to return
Vigor and energy
Is alien to my body
Death will be a relief
From the cancerous thief
Who steals one's life
Cell by cell at a time.

Chapter 6
Living with Cancer, Thinking about the End

This has been a whirlwind month with so many ups and downs, sometimes with the highs and lows occurring in the same day. For example, my youngest son's graduation ceremony from Grade 5. It is a great day for him and his friends and I am proud to see him thriving as he finished Grade 5, recalling earlier years when he didn't like going to school. Today was a special day.

Leaving his graduation, I drove directly to meet my Mom and Dad at the cancer clinic, where Mom had to painstakingly undergo radiation planning, which, like her CT scan a week earlier required her to lay flat on the examination table, which is so painful for her. The oncologist is planning five more radiation treatments to her spine and pelvis, with a 75% chance of successful pain relief. We are concerned at her loss of weight. She remains of sound mind and strong will.

Evening of Life

Cancer cells are racing
Every organ invading
From liver to bone,
No organ left alone
Till every healthy cell
Eventually they kill
Your appetite is no more
Your diet you abhor
Pale and washed out
Looking like a ghost
On the hereafter to ponder
Is there a God, you wonder?
Will it be an easy journey?
With the Lord a meeting?
Or will you rot in hell?
Just pray that god will say
Welcome my child
I will give you a rebirth
For a better resurge
Go, be a humanitarian
Stay a vegetarian
Be a chosen of the Gods
To do good for all.

June 2014:
We were concerned seeing Mom's weight decline although, as always, she remained of sound mind and strong will. She was dismayed to hear of the new metastases spread in her bone, but said she wasn't surprised. She always seems to know when the cancer has started up again or has returned even though my physician Father and I would reassure her that we should not start worrying until the tests were done. She knew, she could feel it.

A waiting game: too sapped of energy to live vigorously, Mom is thinking about past and future, what future? My Mother was a very spiritual person, and this was very comforting to her. A week before she passed away her palliative care physician came to the house and they talked about death and dying and the afterlife. I was sitting beside her holding her hand. She asked him if he thought Heaven existed and if Hitler was denied going to Heaven — they both agreed that he would be denied. She said she wasn't scared of dying, that her beliefs were of reincarnation. This poem captures her thinking:

Only a Few Days Remain

Of my life on earthly domain
How best to spend this precious time
To turn it into a meaningful clime
To make amends for lost time
Is to regret the ride of this life
Atonement will not a heaven gain
For that it is already too late.
Better re-incarnation be the aim
Will prayers carry the day?
Too little too late I say.
What happens to a sinner like me
When they face god in eternity
Be kind o lord I pray
When I face you one day.

Chapter 7
Final Days

Mom wasn't well enough to travel to my house for my son's and my October birthdays. So this year we celebrated by getting take-out fish and chips at Mom and Dad's place. Unfortunately, my Mom is in a lot more pain in her back and is using a cane, hunched over, and there is not much we could do. She is thin but she still tries to get me to eat whenever I visit.

It was hard seeing her; she is stoic but still it didn't seem fair to see her declining and suffering. I silently pledge I will visit her every two days, and I wish I could stay fulltime with her, but I have my own children, my husband, my home, and my work to balance. My husband understood and supported me to do whatever I needed to. Never was this balancing act so many women attempt, more difficult.

October 2014:
It has been a tradition in our family since we moved to rustic, farm country to host a country Thanksgiving dinner. I had been preparing for Thanksgiving with the hopes that my Mother would come, but the night before when I visited her she told me she wasn't sure she would make it, BUT that I still had to have it, that it was good to give thanks and share and celebrate with everyone.

Although I am a fairly even-keeled person, I started to cry uncontrollably, and my Mother told me to stay strong, that I have three children to care for and should not be sad, that I have worked so hard to prepare Thanksgiving for everyone, and it is important to always give to people and to be kind." To comfort me she said, "let's watch *The Wheel of Fortune* together," one of her favourite shows, but I couldn't stop crying. I was so sad to see her so weak and tired and in pain, I was sad to not have her comfort in the future, and to acknowledge that soon she may not be here.

My Father tried to comfort me, and my Mom said I was a wonderful daughter, more than a son could be. Well I will miss her and love her but will do as she says. All the way home on my one hour drive, listening to Cold Play, Sky Full of Stars, I continued to cry. My kids and husband could tell with my puffy red eyes it had been a hard evening, and as I sat down on the couch after the kids went to sleep, my loyal black Labrador Retriever Hannah sat beside me to comfort me. She could always sense when I was sad.

October 20, 2014:
Mom is struggling with increasing pain, slowly unable to get to the bathroom or go upstairs. She is still so loving and kind, still worried about her children and grandchildren, still giving me advice to eat more and not to be too stressed about my daughter at university who has come down with mono. We agree that Mothers can never stop worrying.

My middle child, Anand and I visited on Sunday after his soccer practice. We took treats from Himalaya like samosas, barfi, kheer, roti and daal, and he helped Nani by watering all the plants, and helped Nanu with the water jugs. Mom and Dad are so loving, but it is now hard for them to cope, they need nursing help which I will arrange. Tomorrow is the cancer clinic appointment and I hope there are options for Mom's comfort. Diwali is coming up, but we are too glum to celebrate.

I Watch the Clock

For night to fall
To shut off the world
A wasted life is the word
For my mind's clock
I cannot shut off
The guilt swirls round and round
Like a storm that engulfs ground
Then a prayer rises to the sound
'have mercy, have mercy lord
Forgiveness is the word'
Another chance for a lost soul
I beg, make it my lot
Save my soul, sweet lord.

Chapter 8
The Pain of Cancer is Relentless

October 21, 2014

Mom made a courageous trek to the cancer clinic to have her spine X-ray. I met her with a wheelchair with a soft cushion. She is a real trooper. The receptionist, who loves mom, greeted us and Mom gave her a chocolate bar. The X-ray went smoothly, we had to wait at the lab but eventually got in, the doctors got the blood; everyone was so nice. Overall, not much they can do, no treatments were offered. It was hard for my Mom to say "no hope" when the oncologist told us to plan for palliative care.

It was a solemn rainy day in October. Despite the ominous news we had our usual cheese sandwich in the cancer clinic cafe, lucky to have these times together. I am saddened by Mom's pain and I am wondering: will this be our last meeting here together?

October 30, 2014

Well, Mom is settling into a new routine as her condition deteriorates rapidly. She can only get up to use the washroom, the rest of the time she sits or lies down in bed. She now uses her cane when she walks, stairs are very hard, we must help her to stand, and her legs are too weak to lift her body.

It is unbelievable to see my tough Mother require so much help for activities that were so routine for her. I know she does not like this dependency and is experiencing a lot more pain than she mentions to us.

Last Saturday, when I left their house with my youngest son in tow, Mom got up to see us to the door – it must have been so painful for her to do this – she thanked us for coming and gave us a hug and kiss. Within 10 minutes into our drive back home the car phone rang and my Dad asked us to turn back; Mom had fallen in the kitchen, and he wasn't strong enough to lift her on his own. I prayed on my drive back to their house that Mom didn't break a hip, which would mean a sure trip to the hospital – a place she adamantly did not want to go, it would not offer many options, no indication for surgery and only pain control.

Mom said she was looking in the cupboard and lost her balance and fell backwards. She said she tried to get up, but didn't have the strength, she called out to my Dad who although is hard of hearing came running. Thank the Lord, she was not physically injured, and I was able to lift her back up and to her chair. She was shaken and at that moment we recognized her vulnerability.

November 6, 2014
Today we were at Mom's after I spent the night beside her in the twin bed in her room. The hardest part was seeing her suffering with each step, with each turn in her bed, and when she has to sit up. She has very little strength in her legs and everything is a chore and painful.

I would awaken before her throughout the night, to make sure I could hear her breathing just like I used to do with my newborn babies. I helped her up in the morning, and through her pain she wondered aloud: "am I being punished for something I did in my life, with so much pain?"

She then remarked that she knows how Jesus must have felt on the cross saying, "Oh Father why has thou forsaken me." When we get her up sitting, she seems comfortable and can eat, talk and enjoy the day.

When I left today, she said, "you are my angel, my star."

Pain

Block it out, think no more
Shut the emotional door
Numb the feelings out
Lock the world about
Feel no pain,
Have no fun
Alone and lonely
Forgotten, surely
Feel no pain, be dead
In your unsung end.

Chapter 9

Winter of Life's End

November 2014

Last night I took care of Mom overnight, she was in a hospital bed that we had placed in the dining room of her Georgetown house. It was clear that transferring Mom into bed was hard on her, but once the morphine kicked in, she was peacefully reading her book on Justin Trudeau and was ready for bed by 9:00 PM.

I sat with Dad in the den and we talked about Mom's long journey with cancer: the left mastectomy in 2007, the radiation, the chemotherapy, bone metastases, and then the new cancer requiring a lumpectomy, more radiation, and four months to live when the bone metastases appeared in July 2013, but she has lived beyond that for another 16 months! We are so grateful to have had this extra time, yet it is so hard to see her suffer.

I went to sleep on a floor bed we had made up beside hers and she woke up at 11:30 PM for some turning and pain meds and then slept until 7 am. I was worried, checking her breathing. I even woke her up at 6:30 to be sure she was conscious. After making her drink to take the pain pills, I helped her with the walker to her chair. We spent the morning doing her crossword puzzle, computer work, and then she had visitors, her friend and cousins from the same village in India in which my Mother was born. Later that day the palliative care doctor and nurse came to visit Mom and to ask her questions. It was a privilege to help my Mom in this way. Between three sisters we rotated nights, with one of us staying with Mom each night.

I slept over again two days later, this time bringing a wheelchair to transport her, which helped her a lot. She slept well, I could hear her raspy breathing, but with my stethoscope, her lungs were clear. At 6 am, she woke up worried about how much pain she may have getting up. She waited for the meds to kick in, and we both read the paper and she started the crossword. With the personal support worker's help, we got her to the couch and all day we had the grandkids and families; my husband brought the boys out of school to spend time with Nani, singing songs, sitting with her, it was really special. I can tell she doesn't have long, I'm sad for her suffering, and my anticipated loss. She tells us we are her angels, which says enough.

Saroj knitting

Winter of Life's End

The golden years are ending
As cancer is spreading
From breast to bone
Paining more and more
Analgesic has no control
Piercing pain is the rule
What am I being punished for?
Not keeping my promises to God?
Slow death chemo cannot control
It prolongs life span
Only a bit by bit it can
It is no cure, I can tell
Kills normal cells as well
It opens the door to death
Weakening all body functions
Appetite goes, walk slows
kidneys work slower,
swelling of limbs grow
pain in the liver seat
pigment of hands and feet
darker they grow
day by day dry I grow
creams help no more
cancer is a slow killer at best
no cure for its wiley cells
they resist any chemo
cell by cell they perish
body no longer to cherish
slow but sure they die
one by one they cry
before peeling off
and then it is silence
body works closed in essence
next, cremation to ashes
thrown in holy Ganges

in the age-old Hindu fashion
forever in its water to hasten
so ends life in a flick
golden years thus slink
to bid goodbye there in
for ever to kith and kin.

Nov 19, 2014
I went home for a few hours; an hour each way in a howling wind. I haven't been home much, and I knew my young sons could survive on cereal for only so long. I was able to see the boys and pick up some groceries on my way to pick up my youngest son from soccer. Even though I was very tired, something inside me tugged at me to go return to my parents' house and to be back with my Mother.

    When I reached her house, she had been settled in bed by my sisters, who were ready to go once I arrived. She couldn't sleep during the night. Her heels were hurting, and from time to time she needed water, morphine and Tylenol. She was slightly confused, but then at times very lucid. She would call out, "Sonia!" and also told me, "I wish you the deepest happiness in your life." She asked me if I had eaten and told me, "to go eat Kheer!" She asked me if my sisters were in the house and where my Father was, as if she was seeking to know whether we are all here together. At 4:30 am, she was able to fall asleep – but not for too long.

    I sat with her and gave her some water and warm almond milk sugar drink when she awoke – she enjoys having this by spoon. She told me I must be tired from the past night and said It must be like "being on night duty," but I said, " I would do this for you anytime anyplace – it is my privilege to be here and do this for you." I told her she was the best Mother in the world, and she said again, "you are a wonderful daughter."

    My sisters returned later in the morning, according to all signs, Mom was slipping away. Dad came to her bedside and read Shlokas in Sanskrit which he learned as a child. These prayers and invocations came from *The Gita* – Gandhi's favourite ones – Mom loved hearing these in Sanskrit, and then she repeated the words of the Shlokas. She told my Dad that when she first met him and he passionately told her that he believed in *The Gita*, she knew he was a good man. When he said that, she said, "you were worth waiting for," and she told him, "he was a true kind and gentle man." My sister and I sat beside them with tears rolling down our cheeks.

She was so peaceful and gentle today with Anita, Gita and Dad. Her best friend Saroji visited and they sang the *Hanuman Chalisa* together – Mom tried some of Saroji's Halva and told her she is, "more than a sister."

November 20, 2014
Mom had a hard afternoon on what was to be her last day of life on Earth. The Personal Support Worker was not able to come, and when my sister and I tried to turn mom to change her, she experienced a lot of pain and felt she needed to sit up as she needed to catch her breath. She sat with my sister and I each beside her, she kept saying "Sonia, oh Sonia the pain is excruciating." I felt helpless. We called her nurse and asked her to come earlier than 12 noon, which she did. We were able to change Mom's dressing, providing some relief, but there was such a delay between giving her medication that she agreed to initiate subcutaneous morphine – the nurse needed to call to have them speed up the symptoms management kit, and would return at 4 pm.

After a somewhat restful afternoon with Saroji's visit, it began to snow. Anita, Gita, and Dad went out to do errands. Mom and I stayed together, and I held her hand and talked. When the nurse returned again, we repositioned Mom and needed to change her bedsheets – with her in the bed. Again, Mom felt short of breath and needed to sit up to be comfortable, the nurse, my sister and I helped hold Mom upright, my other sister helped change all of the pillows and linens. Clean bedding, a comfort.

Unfortunately, the subcutaneous morphine had not arrived as the delivery man was caught in snowfall traffic slowdown – the nurse said ideally, we could give a sedative. At one-point, Mom looked directly in to the nurse's eyes and said, "Please be God." I believe because she was suffering so much. We gave Mom her oral meds, and Dad was able to find lorazepam, a sedative which helped relax her and we were able to settle her back into bed. She was so tired from the day that soon she was able to fall asleep as my sister led a chorus of Mom's favorite Christmas Carols; irregular breathing and a deep sleep.

With such an emotional and heart wrenching day for all of us, my Father rallied to help his daughters, and made Kichiri – an Indian rice and daal mix that portends strength to the sick. So, all of us had this and talked between us about the rough day Mom had had. I lay on the floor bed and worked on my laptop, and before I went to sleep, said good night to Mom, gave her a kiss and held her hand. My sister stayed beside me – together to be with Mom.

At midnight my sister was awoken and called me: she had heard Mom throw off her bedcovers. She got Mom some water, but she would not sip via a straw, and she looked into Anita's eyes. I drew up the morphine and injected first 2 mg then the remainder, meanwhile Anita called out that Mom was not swallowing the water – I checked for her pulse and heartbeat and there was nothing… I ran upstairs to get Dad and Gita. They came down, and we stood with Mom and repeated the Gayatri Mantra – an ancient and sacred Sanskrit prayer over and over.

As our Hindu priest said the next day, "We carried her" as her soul lifted off to her next life. We were numbed and bewildered. I spoke to the family doctor and the nurse on the phone – and then called nursing care who came to do the official pronouncement. The whole night we sat with Mom and held her hand – we were in shock, half believing she was only sleeping. Dad slept on the floor bed next to us, he needed a small sleeping pill and slept a bit. In the morning we called our husbands and spoke to each one of our kids – each conversation was painful and filled with sorrow.

Death

Face to face with death
A relief from painful health
Where will the soul wander?
A lost spirit without anchor
Will the gods give it shelter
Or will they shut their door
To a wastrel and a sinner
Peaceful end one longs for
Pain free, without struggle
Know not what happens
The last breath into thin air
The soul into another new babe
Hopefully into a fair home
Pious and godly do-gooders.

At 8 am, the funeral home came to take our dear Mom from the house. Again, we all prayed with her. Dad read Sanskrit Shlokas and we read her poetry. When they came, I wouldn't look and I cried with Anita, while Dad and Gita went outside and watched as they drove Mom away. It was only then that they too cried for our loss.

Chapter 10

Mother's Wish

November 20 – 22

The time after Mom passed away is a blur for me, but I have flashes of moments from these days from time to time. A combination of wondering, "how did I make it through those days?" and reflections of the outpouring of love and kindness from so many people who came together with our family to bid farewell to my Mother.

The family gathered in Georgetown and being together helped us all. In the few days after my Mother's passing, there were lots of tearful phone calls with friends and relatives. We organized the visitation and funeral rather quickly, my eldest sister leading the charge. The grandkids worked on putting a slide show and poster of many pictures of their Nani.

Anita and I went with Mom's best friend Saroji to the funeral home to dress Mom. This was very hard: to see Mom, to hold her hardworking and guiding hand for the last time. The finality of death and of our journey began to set in. We chose her 50th wedding anniversary sari, which she loved: the beautiful orange (a holy colour) and cream-gold in which to dress her. Saroji led us in saying prayers and we together worked to dress Mom in her sari. She looked beautiful and peaceful, but the moment was overwhelming and surreal.

Myles, my children, and my sister's family all came together at the Georgetown house, the place we all had met every Sunday afternoon for the past 20 years. This home was my Mother's palace, a warm and inviting, homey-home, and it was this strong sense of her embedded into this house that made us all just want to stay in the house, and which made us feel like Mom was still with us.

Just before we left the house for the funeral home at 6pm, we were amazed to see that my Mother's sister had arrived from

London, England! Mom would have been so happy to have her with us, and together we went to the funeral home. The evening was long, we had many, many visitors coming to pay their respects to Mom and to our family. There were many beautiful flowers from many of our friends and family. I left after speaking with so many treasured friends. I had to catch myself as I instinctively wanted to go home and tell Mom all about it.

My Mother collected beautiful things, from furniture, to art, to porcelain figurines, to books – tons of books from her favorite biographies, to spiritual books. We had everything from Hindu scriptures, to Koran, to Bibles, stories of crucifixion, Jesus-Krishna comparison books and more. My Mother's kitchen and sitting room was crowded with plants, pictures of her children and grandchildren, and paintings. My Mother was firm to us on very few things – they were few items but clear words – always stick together as close family – no fighting over material goods – she had carefully and equally divided between her three daughters her jewelry from generations before her that she had inherited. I remember that night very clearly, and she said, "but the love I leave behind is for the family to unite on inheritance. No fighting, honour this wish of mine."

In addition, there was to be no selling her books or furniture. No fanfare, a private funeral, that is all she said to us.

Here are her words:

Last Will and Testament

These collectibles of mine,
Silver and china so fine
Are there for the picking,
Are there for the taking.
After I am gone, my child
Obey this wish of mine
No bickering, no fight
Take whatever you like
Share and share alike
Remember not to fight
For my soul it will bite
In the tomb's dark night
Honour this edict of mine
Love each other, no strife
In ups and downs of life
Love and love alike
these worldly goods of mine
are mere objects of a kind
but the love I leave behind
is for the family to unite
on inheritance, no fight
honour this wish of mine
With manners that are refined
You shall have peace of mind
Under the grace of the divine
Honour this last wish of mine.

November 22: Funeral day
My family and I stayed in Georgetown Friday night with Dad. In the morning my dear Dad in his own shock and grief carried on my parents' tradition and made us pancakes!

We went to the funeral home together by 10:30 in the morning. The service itself went very well, it was very sad and many tears – the tears would come and go throughout the morning with little warning. The grandchildren all spoke beautifully as a tribute to their dear Nani who took care of each one of them with such tender loving care.

Dad's idea of having coffee and sandwiches afterwards for all of our family and friends was excellent as we got to speak to everyone who attended the funeral one-on-one. Finally, the grandsons and husbands honoured Mom by carrying her casket into the hearse and together we travelled to the cremation site. Despite the cold warehouse feeling at the site it did have the sense of finality.

A sad ending to a long few weeks, and for my Mother – seven years of her valiant battle with cancer.

Our Days are Done

We have had our fun
Adieu my friend
This is the end
It was a great ride
In good company beside
So much was given
An earthly heaven
So little returned
Goodbye my friend
Till we meet again
Friends for ever to remain
In some never neverland
Along each other to stand.

Chapter 11

Angels

One year later, November 2015
Today, a Monday, I rush through the hospital to begin clinic, the first patient is waiting. As I pass through the long hallway of the hospital, I spot an elderly couple, holding a piece of paper and looking lost. "Excuse me," they say, "can you tell us where the second floor, yellow section is? We have an appointment."

I thought back to the multitude of appointments to which I led my Mother through this very hospital. We would comment to each other that the hospital is like a maze, and my Mother always said she was lucky to have me as her guide – I had gone to medical school here, finished my residency here and knew my way around easily.

"Follow me," I said, "I am heading in that direction." I guided them to the place of their appointment and wished them a good day and good luck with the upcoming surgery. As I walked away, I heard them say, "wasn't that so kind of her to do that for us?" I smiled to myself, they couldn't know what I was thinking, and how I wished I could be back in the days of walking with my Mother, but I knew my Mother would be smiling down upon me – nodding "Yes be kind, and help each other."

Angels

Angels, angels, where are you
For miracles, I thank you
God sent you my way
A miracle to brighten my day
I found what I was searching
In full view it was scintillating
As if out of the blue
It dropped in full view
All in seconds seven
O! From lord's seventh heaven
It was a wish come true
My golden angel carried it through.

Epilogue

December 20, 2016

Yesterday I went with my Father and older sister to a meeting of the poetry group that my Mother started. She loved this group with a passion. She quietly recruited her poet soldiers and every second week they would convene to write and share poetry.

Today, we gathered at another woman's house and they started with a toast to "their mentor," "to Saroj." I felt their warmth and solidarity around me, I felt my Mother's warmth within me. She would have loved this get-together. We reminisced and as I was having lunch, my Mom's friend Helen beside me leaned over and said, "I imagine your Mother has gathered all of the saints together in heaven and they are writing poetry, I look forward to joining the group when I get there."

Each woman had a memory to share: how Mom was a cornerstone to them, how she was such a gracious yet strong woman, how she would marvel about Donald Trump's election if she were here, how she was a pioneer, an inspiration.

At the time I imbibed their praise of my Mother, but now as I write, tears roll down my face. I miss my Mother's soft touch and gracious leadership. I try and emulate her being, her spirit. She had so much humility, but curiously would belittle her own accomplishments, calling her life a failure, saying she didn't accomplish anything, yet she exhibited all of the elusive traits that we all struggle and hope to achieve in our lifetimes: humility, wisdom, grace. I was born lucky, lucky to have her divine love.

Losing the love of a Mother is like no other loss. It is a deep, heart wrenching pain, like a house's foundation being shaken in an earthquake. Whether the house can still stand is testament to the resilience instilled within its beams. My Mother spent her life quietly instilling such resilience in her children and grandchildren. She lived as a role model for us, being immensely kind and caring and continually sprinkling us with advice to live by, the importance of hard work, doing one's duty, and being truthful and kind.

In the days, months, and now years, since her passing, her words both spoken and written are a comfort to me. The kind and deeply heartfelt care and love from others has been a crutch to keep me going. I realize in my work and through my friends and acquaintances that many of us have lost loved ones to cancer, it is a difficult and painful journey for us all.

I hope that reading of our experience and hearing of my Mother's journey with cancer provides an opportunity for reflection on your own journey, perhaps providing some comfort.

A poem written by my youngest son (Age 11), read at her Funeral:

Nani — written by Sachin Sergeant

Nani, the best grandma ever/
Always gives her best try she can endever/
A great doctor and also a poet
Nani will always be heroic/
Also she was a successful medical doctor
And she has created a family with an incredible/
always supplying us with toblerones and ginger ale/
nani has become injured and frail
nani we will always remember
a sad month this month of november
always keeping a positive mentality
never getting mad or making a catastrophe
Always happily never ~~sad or~~ there must be a strategy/
~~Delightful~~ It is a sad time so much tragedy
that all of this happened so tragically
In the end Nani has lived up
to infinity her life has been
a victory.

Saroj Ram, sitting at her computer writing her poetry at her home in Georgetown.

om
shanti
shanti
shanti

www.ingramcontent.com/pod-product-compliance
Lightning Source LLC
Chambersburg PA
CBHW071254070526
44583CB00017B/2465